The LAW *of* TRULY LARGE NUMBERS

PITT
POETRY
SERIES

TERRANCE HAYES
NANCY KRYGOWSKI
JEFFREY MCDANIEL

Editors

Published by the University of Pittsburgh Press, Pittsburgh, Pa., 15260

Copyright © 2025, James Kimbrell

All rights reserved

Manufactured in the United States of America

Printed on acid-free paper

10 9 8 7 6 5 4 3 2 1

ISBN 13: 978-0-8229-6737-8

ISBN 10: 0-8229-6737-5

Cover art and design by Alex Wolfe

For My Children
ALLI, SOFIA, DARBI, AND THOMAS

CONTENTS

I

II

III

IV

For now we see only a reflection as in a mirror;
then we shall see face to face.

—I Corinthians 13:12

SELF-PORTRAIT AS THIEF CONFESSING AFTER THE FACT

At Jr. Mart, one eye on the mirror, I
wedge my meal between skin and waistband.
A quick shake of my leg and the microwave
cheeseburger, cold as Nebraska, slips
down my thigh behind my knee, trending
south to the elastic cuff of my sweats.
No one suspects an ankle. And my ankle's fat
when I step into the parking lot, not
looking back, two ounces of frozen beef
with its dinky stamp of American cheese
and a few gelid squares of diced onion
thawing slowly against my calf. July
sunlight on the gas pumps. Concrete dotted
with dark wads of abandoned gum.

MAKING A TURKEY SANDWICH FOR MIKHAIL BARYSHNIKOV

It doesn't matter how high you lift your leg. The technique is about transparency, simplicity and making an earnest attempt.

—Mikhail Baryshnikov, *Baryshnikov at Work*, 1978.

Because he finally appeared during my shift
and I could see him beyond my prep window
and the cold display and the cash register
sitting at the four-top with Jessica Lange
and their daughter, Alexsandra, I made an earnest
attempt to slice the sunflower wheat bread
with disinterested grace, to keep the crust
unbroken before layering the smoked meat
with lettuce, mayo, avocado, and three strips
of applewood bacon, then cutting
the whole into halves, perfectly tooth-picked
gourmet doppelgangers of abundance and,
one hoped, restraint. Fingers hooked in my
apron collar, I watched as this table of three
who represented a ridiculously large share
of Earth's talent and beauty were served
their sandwiches, or as I liked to think of them,
their edible sculptures. I did not walk out
to the forbidden gleaming customer area
to introduce myself, a fan, an aspiring poet,
a dishwasher and slicer of serious bread.
I was not the Baryshnikov of poetry.

I was not even the Baryshnikov of sandwiches.
And a family deserves to eat in peace, and I
deserved to watch them, or I didn't, but watched
anyway, though not ostentatiously. It wasn't
easy to slice a fresh round of focaccia
when I wanted to set forth in my hair-net
and scream "Mikhail! Mikhail! I'm so happy
you got free from nasty old Russia where a 5'5" male
could never dance the lead!" In my salty halo,
in my cloud of bread steam, I recalled
childhood visions of an airborne jeté
over pool halls and pine-tops, the water tower
a train set figurine in the air beneath me.
Of course, like most boys in Mississippi
I was herded decidedly away from ballet
toward football, hunting. I wonder, how many
poets are would-be dancers? Name one
good poem that doesn't long for escape.
After they finished, napkins on plates,
Baryshnikov's crumbs were everyday crumbs.
Nor was the silverware infected with
greatness. Such are the mysteries of genius
and mastication. The oven bell rang, as did
the order bell and the dish bell, all the bells
that said the meal is ready, and the cake. Still,

with damp cloth and bucket, I stepped out
and took my time clearing their table.

MEDITATIONS ON A BOWL MADE FROM THE WALNUT TREE UPENDED IN LAST YEAR'S HURRICANE

1.

Sober, my dad liked to read
    beneath the tree that the bowl
        used to be. One day I climbed
           the ladder with a bag of seed

to the bird feeder that hung
    from its lowest branch. My dad
        looked up from his book and said,
           "You're about to bust your ass."

2.

The nuts were inedible, plagued
    with webworms, but the wood
        is this chocolatey swirl of storm wounds
           and bird dreams that I turned

by lathe and gouge and chisel
    into this otherworldly vessel, oiled
        and buffed to a dark glimmer, filled with
           stamps, screws, capo, spare change.

3.

It's hard to impress a ghost. Once,

    I made my father a clay ashtray.

        It was impossible to clean and

            went down the drain in ash-stained

clumps. If my father were alive

    to see this bowl, I think he'd give it

        to his AA group that it might brim

            with dollar bills, a coffee-fund overflow.

4.

And then money would, in fact, grow

    on a tree, even if the tree is gone.

        The roots still bulge beyond

            the ferns that circle the stump

that shows the sixty widening years

    it took to turn a single nut

        into a force for green, throwing

            shade, gathering up the weather.

5.

Bowl, you are not my father. If you

> were a door to the next world, my dad

> > would've hitch-hiked to the dog tracks

> > > with all your money. Still, with the whorls

and loops of your grain's

> figuration, you might be a large catfish

> > nosing toward the light, looking up

> > > at a bug striding across a stage of water.

6.

A bowl worthy of Greek salad

> at the thunder table of a famished Zeus

> > whose brother rules the second

> > > life where perchance some measure

of the tree still grows, if upside

> down, rending walnuts gratefully

> > cracked in a windless realm,

> > > that bounty of glorious shadows.

HEY DEWAYNE

—Reunion, Class of '85

Didn't you shoot the water tower with a dart gun?
Didn't you join the Masons? Didn't we walk down
the swamp road and spew pot smoke into each other's faces

concurrent with hyperventilation? Didn't I fall down
for a minute, then wake in awe of Def Leppard,
loblolly pines like compass needles fucked with

by the wind-magnet? Didn't we go to three funerals
that Saturday? Didn't we sit in the abandoned
tractor trailer shifting the dead gears? Didn't they

sound like a hailstorm of horse teeth? Didn't the well water
taste like matchheads? Wasn't our team sponsored
by the sawed-off light of the turpentine factory?

Didn't our coach point to the example with a busted
car antenna? Didn't we ride your Kawasaki in the rain
all the way to Turkey Fork in December? Didn't the gray sky

leave a skid mark on the ridgeline? Wasn't there
supposed to be a bonfire at the bridge, but the boat-
ramp gate was welded shut, and the weedy beach

was empty, but for an X of smoldering driftwood?

DECOUPAGE

Like the valley between speech and thought,
like a yellowbird's shadow, like a word
                without an ego, like the routine distance
between truth and Richard Millhouse Nixon,
        my mother and I cut pictures out of magazines
of the things we wanted and glued them
                to things we had. It's not easy riding a bike
        stuck to the side of a coffee can. Where's
Jimmy? He's in a tree house glued to a rock. A yacht
        anchored off Saint-Tropez, brunch
                in the Piazzale Michelangelo, pigeons
        in a flurry around a crowd approaching
the Taj Mahal, all adorned our pièce
        de résistance—a once-tweed valise
parked by the door as if in a rush of windswept
        arrival. Because some substitutes are like
no other. Because the tableau is easier to touch
                than the world it suggests. Because who
        doesn't need an unrequited forever-ized
with Elmer's and a clear coat of nail polish?
        How sweet the fumes, how fleet
                the surfboard on my jelly-jar pencil cup.

WATCHING NASCAR ON THE ANNIVERSARY OF MY SISTER'S DEATH

Dear God, like an invisible race car at Talladega,
you accelerate my confusion. I presented unto you

my graveside face, my wood-chopping holler, but I
get it: my sister exists on a different channel.

No matter how much Anaconda Aluminum Foil
I wrap around the rabbit ears, I can't pick up her signal.

Then she appears in a dream to say, "If you
tell me your dreams, we can meet in our dreams,

and tell each other about that." But I dream
I'm sunbathing in a ditch with a gas can full of lotion.

I dream I'm swinging nun-chucks of dynamite
and no one offers me a ride. I dream Farmer Wind

pulls his cargo of clouds with a string tied
to a combine harvester, then my tooth falls out.

I dream the city is a mind of roads in relation
to what once grew there, my sister nowhere in sight.

Thusly, Dear Lord, you make as much sense
as an upgrade to Formica. Still, we are drawn to you

like nails to a magnet pulled across a sawdust
subfloor. Still, we conduct ourselves beneath

a sky-colored punch bowl, ready for your cup.

A DAY IN SEPTEMBER

Nothing monumental about a dog bounding after his own tail,
   all slobber and fury in the weedy yard across from the red light,
      but when I looked out of my preschool principal's idling car
         on our way to the hospital to get my eyelid stitched up,

when I looked out the window with my one good eye, and the dog
   spun himself into a blurry cyclone in perfect sync with ABBA's
      "Fernando"— O, the disco in all things, the unorchestrated
         sky-parting joyance of that sudden symmetry walloped me,

and I had no words for what I saw, the pure shine of the absurd
   like a giant lasso orbiting the blue Pontiac where we sat
      in silence, but for the radio, waiting for the light at West Capital

and Rose, dried blood stuck to my brow from the playground
   culvert that I tried to jump through earlier that morning
      when I was a colt running with horses across the Bouie River.

WEST JACKSON TOPOGRAPHY

*Justices William O. Douglas, William J. Brennan Jr, Byron R. White and Thurgood
Marshall dissented. Marshall, a Negro, said that when Jackson officials "denied a single
Negro child the opportunity to go swimming simply because he is a Negro, rights guaranteed to
that child by the 14th Amendment were lost."*

—*The Clarion Ledger*, Jackson, Mississippi, June 15, 1971

[THE LAKE]

Because Jackson was a police state with surprisingly few police,
Poseidon of the Confederacy did not surge up
from the tentacled deep of Livingston Park Lake
and look askance at an integrated citizenry
splashing around with blow up floats in the familiar presence
of each other's children. Nope: the city elders
closed the lake tighter than a padlocked paddleboat,
that clear serene ten-acre lake with its postcard island
and platform high dive where no one
backflipped or belly-flopped post Jim Crow.

[THE LAWSUIT]

Comes down from the choppy shores of the United States Supreme Court
like a stone-cold tablet cut from the mountain Jackson doesn't have: in
the matter of *Palmer v. Thompson*, 403 U.S. 217, the city may have closed
swimming holes to avoid integration, but said places of aquatic respite are
in violation of no federal order as they no longer exist. A closed swimming
area treats no one preferentially. Black or white: THOU SHALT NOT!

[THE WHITE FEAR]

The hippy white trash Negro and other communist swimmers of Jackson
    are sweating
        on the high bluffs foaming
beneath the diving boards hysterical to get wet a clear threat to civil order
    bound
        to culminate

in cultural disintegration and the inevitable blendation of untold fluids and
    follicles
        and rhythms pernicious
for which we can ill afford to provide floaties to say nothing of the exorbitant
    cost
        of ammunition

billy-clubs patrol cars German shepherds evacuation of livestock at the
    fairgrounds and
        price of imprisonment
in said facilities soon to be brimming with mulattos in swim trunks and
    where
        will the goats,

where will the cows go?

[QUESTIONS FROM THE FUTURE]

Instead of letting us swim together, the city built a kiddy train around the lake as if that would slake our need for immersion, but why would you call a train built for children *The Chimneyville Choo-Choo*? The newspapers renamed antebellum Jackson "Chimneyville" after Grant's troops discovered a stash of rum and matches and torched nearly everything within drunk-marching distance to the Bowen House where the General himself entertained Northern dignitaries in the fire light of the burning city on an otherwise mild evening in May, 1863. Why not just call the kiddy train, *The Ongoing Civil War*, or *The Train on Which You Cannot Swim*?

[THE TRAIN]

Hurry if you want to catch
the Chimneyville Choo-Choo!
Faster than a caterpillar,
lumbering toward the library,
slinking past the Doric gazebo
and its fluted roof that beams
like a pawn shop Rolex
on the wrist of civic pride.
Onward chugs our half-pint
express, our loco locomotive,
nine cars long, two seats wide,
blowing hard its pre-recorded
whistle. Look, ducks! Black
and white, patrolling the shore, all
waddle and quack for a saltine
cracker! Sad boo-boo prize,
the only thing this train
does with a modicum of alacrity
is bore the hell out of us.

[THE BOREDOM]

Daryl said it sucked, and I said it too,
sitting on the hill watching the train enter
and exit its covered wooden bridge
like a python that ate a pig that ate a forest.
Our cause neither history nor justice,
we laid long an ellipsis of rocks
on one modest stretch of Choo Choo track.
Like robbers in a dusty Western,
we ducked inside the hollow trunk
of a zombified oak that was not
well ventilated and which Daryl said
smelled like white people. I smelled
myself to check. We peeked out,
petrified with excitement when
the train shot around the corner
at a blistering speed of maybe
three miles per hour. Neither engine
nor caboose jumped the rails or rolled
downhill in flames. A disgruntled
park employee in engineer's hat
disembarked, cleared the rocks,
his passengers confused, perhaps,
but not fearful, not clutching

their purses or passing out. We tried,
me and Daryl, but we found
no trouble and did not tell our fathers
after sprinting the five blocks
back to Clinton Avenue
where they never once stood
in the buggy gloam
drinking tallboys in paper sacks,
man-gabbing from either side
of the cyclone fence
that separated the grassless dirt
of our respective yards.

EASY NOW

Galloping a wide arc up the sidewalk, a little girl
slaps her hips to make the racket of hooves. It's early
winter and her winded mother, who is not a horse,
finally catches up, apologizes for her daughter,

the child whinnying to a cantor up ahead. The mother
explains that this equine display has haunted
their every horseless day since her husband, the girl's
father, died with no warning. I think of November,

carrying my mother's ashes into the funeral home—
I passed a group of mourners heading for their cars
and wondered, what are they dressed up for? It
had stopped existing for me, the grief of others.

No well like farewell. No deeper drink. The woman
says her husband was not diseased, not very old.
Nor was he known to ever feed, groom, or even
speak in a calming voice to a horse. But he's gone.

And his daughter, her mane unbraided, steps
toward us, sniffing the air, one hoof forward,
testing the grass, as if just back from the free-range
skies of Montana, unsure of human company.

THE LAW OF TRULY LARGE NUMBERS

With a large enough sample, any outrageous thing is likely to happen.

—Persi Diaconis and Frederick Mosteller, "Methods for Studying
Coincidences," *Journal of the American Statistical Association*

Earth is so heavy with people, my love,
we've doubled our numbers since my arrival.
You can still fit twenty humans into a Volkswagen Beetle,
but I worry, will there be enough seatbelts
for our four children? What if civilization
bottoms out backing down our driveway?
Or you can populate two New York Cities
with people that share your birthday.
Isn't that, and that, and that a coincidence?
A miracle might strike at any moment.
Everything rare is well done. Everyone compares
their lottery winnings. So long, religion.
down the road, rabbit's foot. But even
in a world of colossal, humongous, truly superb,
blimp-sized numbers, my love, we're
exactly two people. And when we sleep,
despite what my snoring might suggest,
I am only one man. And of that night
I proposed with Chablis and pawn shop diamond
beneath the walnut tree, and you said yes,
I'll say this: quantity only betters the structure
of affection, the architecture of surprise.

As when you step from the shower
and search for your towel even though
I've hidden it for the millionth time
so that I might behold you searching
for your towel until you finally ask, "Hey, have you
seen my towel?" At which point
I jump to the rescue with dry, fluffy,
wondrous towels worthy of Nefertiti,
and the whole morning smells like sweet pea
and violet body wash, lavender and citrus
anti-frizz conditioner, and this is only
the first hour of the day. I'm one
timeline away from figuring out
when the odds kicked in, how I found you.
It's so crowded, my love, and we've all
been mistaken for someone else
with the same first name and a one-digit difference
in our social security numbers. If only
we could hold a truly large mirror
up to Earth, we could at least gain the illusion
of spaciousness. This would also solve
the problem of surveillance. Everybody
making love outside, looking up
at themselves making love in the sky.

GOOD GRIEF

When someone posts on our neighborhood group
that she's downsizing and needs a good home
for a dozen pelts of her former pets (some frozen,
some laundered) I feel a little lost. What else

have I missed? When did this kick off?
Was I wrong to bury Toby and Buddy Dog
along the back fence where once they ran,
barking at the neighbor's malamute,

each grave marked with a paver stone
the grass creeps over, which I pull by hand
lest the mower blade cough up sparks?
It's true. I'd love to pet them both again.

But they crossed the river with coats on
and now I have living pets that lounge
around my desk like Roman Senators
on holiday, well-fed, arguably over-loved,

frequently spoken to in sentences as if
a response might follow in perfect Latin.
They sleep on the bed, under the bed,
beside the bed, my Siamese lick-sanding

my nostrils until I rise and fill her bowl
with a morning's worth of Meow Mix.
Our love might last forever, but we won't.
Centuries of scheming have rendered

no footpath around the mighty Styx.
And most taxidermy is in decidedly bad taste.
So, after grooming their death coats
for decades, our neighbor resolves

it's time to let go, and that others might
dream of stroking the fur of dead pets
they never knew. I understand nothing,
except that maybe our neighbor is due

a wellness check, and me too. There's
no end to where grief might lead us—
booze, gambling, brushing the dead,
keeping them here with us, making

a second life of what they leave behind
because even a single hair evokes
their presence, their breath, their wait
at the door before we get home.

PORTRAIT OF CHILD AS CITY PLANNER

Under the house in the crawl space with its cool air,
its interstate of pipes, nails jutting out of joists,
empire of soft dirt and tunnels I dug with a spoon,
I had a dump truck whose little man
drove a few feet before backing up, lifting his payload
into a mound, a monument for the future citizenry
of the kingdom that populated my hours. I'd say
things ran well there, as municipalities go.
The bus ran to the skate rink. Fathers didn't drink
until after work. No one turned up the volume,
or the Valium. No one spent Christmas in the nuthouse
with Breakdown Santa. Even when it rained,
it was dry in my town, but as one man's sky
is another man's floor, it thundered when my dad
journeyed to the fridge, my mom shuffling
on her feet at the kitchen sink, my sister taking roll
in her pretend classroom, stomping around,
calling my name. There's no road or paint-splattered
porch steps leading back to my family and their
many imperfections, which I never planned for.
I never built a cemetery. I built a grocery store,
a courthouse, a red, white, and blue rocket slide
in the playground behind the petting zoo.

GROUP MEDITATION, CAMP BRATTON-GREEN, 1978

The camp counselor's voice
was sun-shot molasses—*invite
the light*, she said, so I let it
ebb up my knuckles and elbows
until warmth washed over
my entire torso like sunset
on a pocked brick wall, and I
became that light—sort of—face up
and afloat on the chapel floor.
Gong rung, I was the last
camper to slowly—mindfully—
open my eyes in the supine
position of renewed awareness,
surprised to find the others
tittering, gawking in my
direction. Clearly, my sweatpants
had tent-poled, campsite
of my own unplanned erection.
Could it be that my ego
had departed through my penis?
My pecker rigid with my spirit's
activation? And where
were you, O Angel of Tumescence,
in my red-faced hour? Why
not appear in the rafters

and proclaim readiness
the greatest virtue, or at least
trumpet the relative
innocence of certain pubescent
reactions? Thereafter, I
was dubbed "Hard-on Boy."
But the real growth came
after the ribbing: I started
not to care. What could I say?
Sometimes a kid relaxes.

SELF-PORTRAIT, BASIC TRAINING, FORT MCCLLELAN

Each M-16 site adjusted to the cheeks and jowls of its respective Private, it was my task to paint numbers on the rifle stocks between the safety and butt plate corresponding to its shooter so that each solider was issued the same rifle each day. A bottle of Liquid Paper for paint, my brush was stiff and dry, splayed like a fanned turkey tail. I added a dash of water. What a thinned-out mess I made. The numbers dripped down the stocks like milk might run down a windowpane. Drill Sergeant shook his head in disgust, sent me to edge the sidewalk in front of the barracks, which I did on hand and knee, pulling the grass in small clumps. I did not sprout wings and hover above the barracks. Nor did I challenge Drill Sergeant to a haiku contest. I woke up at three A.M. the next day like all the other grunts getting screamed at, rushing around for that morning's shit, shower, and shave, a five-minute affair at best, Drill Sergeant banging on a garbage can lid. Then, my breath in the dirt of the parade field where we did mountain-climbers and push-ups in the dark, grass still damp to the touch. I kept my chin in my chest and did my best to do what I was told, Drill Sergeant haloed in the field light with his loud speaker barking orders atop

> the tower we'd soon
> repel down—ants on the run
> from a garden hoe.

SPACETIME BLUES

Because spacetime may be curved, a time traveler may find himself revisiting an event in his own past even though, from his perspective, he has been traveling toward the future all the time.

—J. Richard Gott, *Time Travel in Einstein's Universe*

1.

Because my telescope exaggerates the optics inherent in perception itself,
I'm never sure what I'm looking at.

Is that Cassiopeia, or my eyelash?
Is that Ursa Minor, or my sister jumping her skateboard off a plywood ramp?

"It is not good for the wanderer to stray in that infinity," said Johannes Kepler.
A straight line moving in one direction

                    might never return to Earth.

A self-addressed stamped envelope could travel endlessly in space.

A body could wander off-course in the sheer square footage of night sky,
get stranded in the starry unknown

                    between Poplarville and Mars.

Like my sister once told me, pointing to the moon,

                    "That's where we're standing."

2.

We were hanging out in Liz Trotter's front yard. We were spinning in circles
for the cheap buzz.

Liz's father came back from the war with one arm. Our dad returned
with schizophrenia, so we had a lot in common.

Unable to reconcile my lust for infinity with my fear of formlessness, I fell
to the grass. I watched the stars spin to a dizzy rest.

I said the stars are on fire *and* in space.
That's a double whammy!

My sister said there's nothing out there that's not in the cells of a single
human hair.

What about in a banana peel on the porch steps?
What about a dog's tongue licking up spilt Dr. Pepper
from an unswept sidewalk?

3.

Left to themselves, the senses form an egg shape, a limit around the body.
Magnified two hundred times,

        behold: galactic dust, moon pastures, daylight on Venus.

Travelling toward the future, we might arrive at the past.

The grown-ups were in the house drinking beer.
Forty years later the house is still there.

If time were distance, which it is, and distance can be traversed, which it can

then I'm one spaceship away from my family,
good doctor. One spaceship away.

We were hanging out in Liz Trotter's front yard,
We were laying in the itchy grass,

        swatting mosquitoes, naming stars we couldn't see.

FIRST DAY, MIDDLE SCHOOL

I wave from the goodbye area
reserved for the wearers of pantsuits
and pressed slacks, keepers of fobs
and lipsticks. Coffee breath. I wave
and wave as if toward the bannered deck
of a cruise ship. My daughters don't
quite skip. They almost float. Then
they vanish ahead of their paisley-print
backpacks. Racing forms. Dog tracks.
That's how my father would follow
a morning like this. Not to hedge
his bets, but that luck might swell
before it swerves, might rain paid bills
and Old Milwaukee, whole cases
of King Dongs and academic success.
There's a horn honking contest
in the drop-off lane, our town's only
traffic jam, courtesy of parents
too rushed to park. I think of my father
holding up the line at Bill's Mini Mart,
raking a house key across a scratch-off card,
then one more, then another, until
the poor woman behind him drops
her cat food on the gummed-up floor
and walks out. Little did she know

that the world was my father's casino,
each dawn a link in the gold chain
of his omnipresent quasi-Vegas. Progress
dictates that I drive to my office
where no unloved greyhounds
chase a painted rabbit. My bet: the stapler
sits to the left of the pencil cup. Still,
it screws me up, what can happen
on any day at any school: lunatics
with guns. Perverts with cameras.
Bullies. Pink Eye. Somewhere
in the red brick building, my daughters
are making new friends, setting out
on a path of neat, orderly rows.
Is it too much to hope for, God
of Lotto and roulette, source
of all pawnshops and wind, natural
or pumped-in, whose spirt moves
through cafeterias, science class,
and slot machines alike, is it
too much for you to protect them?
Blessed is the freedom to ask.
Blessed is the freedom to make
a hard right for the Davis County
Greyhound Track, for the bag

of peanuts and racing card and the back-
stretch rush of almost winning.

PORTRAIT OF SADIE IN THREE WORLDS

My basset hound has cataracts.
She slips on stairs, can't control
where she squats. When I call,
she looks in the opposite direction.

And yesterday, my wife found
one of Sadie's molars on the kitchen floor.
The vet says she has maybe half
a year. I try to clear a space in my

heart's calendar, my mind's list
of days I don't look forward to.
I buy soft chews, which Sadie stashes
inside the couch, doggy rich. Soon

as she wakes, I walk her out
to the yard. She stops, sniffs
the air for minor changes. Hint
of neighbor dog, trace of fox.

Will she sense me from above
on that day when she passes?
Will she see me at the fence line
with my shovel and prayer?

Will she return to my sister
whom she slept beside the morning
my sister died? I walk Sadie
back inside. Once she's pointed

in the right direction, she heads
for the kitchen, toenails
clicking on the hardwood floor.
Now, her floppy ears still wet

from the water bowl, she sleeps
behind my chair, a bright youth
and a fearsome hunter in a dream
that makes her twitch, makes

her jowls rustle out a muffled
half-bark behind the jackrabbit
she chases, zig-zagging
through bull thistle, wild grape.

FLEA TRAP

And in this flea our two bloods mingled be . . .

—John Donne

1.

When M____ shuffles into the madhouse lobby—no earrings, no laces in her shoes—it seems inopportune to mention the pan of water and liquid Dawn that I rigged up on our bedroom floor, how the lamp shines above it like a lover's moon over Pascagoula, but when fleas leap for the heat of the bulb, the great arc of their adventure lands them in the pan where they bog down in the slimy pull of soap.

2.

Since the voices told M____ to check herself in, neither of us knows if or when we'll stroll down our busted sidewalk between the blighted dogwoods, just me and M____ and M____'s favorite flea, the flea who loved her when she flushed her meds, flea whom she walked around our neighborhood on a leash of thread, cussing out old ladies if they stepped too close, and M____'s flea cussing too, though only she and dolphins could hear his high-pitched cry, his tiny complaint.

3.

I don't tell M____ that Mr. Mattuse will not replace the AC that fell out of the window when the window fell out, just as he refuses to bomb beneath the house where the infestation began in a dank oasis of sandy soil and leaky pipes. M____ reports a surprisingly tasty tapioca. Says the orderlies unraveled her French braids to prevent self-harm, which seems odd given that she spent half a day weaving a hanging basket in occupational therapy. Fleas and love, love and fleas. There are two things driving me crazy, and only one of them is crazy.

4.

In lieu of M____, I sing to the fleas. I whistle as they spin in their soapy orbits. I hum a lullaby to the fleas decked out in their watery death boats about which I am starting to feel a creeping guilt. Soon, I'll get lonely and have to perform CPR on a flea I nearly watch drown before I come to my senses and fish him out, and his brothers and sisters, his aunts and cousins, and his pets, and his pets' fleas. I shall lie on the floor naked and let them feast on my elbows and knuckles until they are the size of average humans.

5.

Bottoms up, I say to M____ when the nurse rounds the corner with her clipboard and dose. To good hygiene, M____ says, then burps, which magnetizes me, makes me long for a month of kisses. But there are rules. Rules in lieu of sanity. Traps for fleas, rules for kisses. For instance, I don't ask M____, why did you abandon me? Was I the heat, or the hound beneath the flea-bait porch?

6.

Nor do I offer the letter that began, Dear M____, I moved to Virginia. Nor the one that started, Dear M____, I paid the rent. Dear M____, the stuck fleas kick in tight, gluey circles before settling into their new look: flecks of pepper in the dishwater of circumstance. Still, when the nurse takes her smoke break, we slip like newlyweds down the long hall toward the barred window, the linoleum squeaky, buffed to an antisceptic mirror-like glow. Excluding the taste of each other's lips, neither of us knows what to expect.

7.

What I tell M____: I wrote a poem about a squirrel and a pillow case, walked to Delchamps for free coffee, Hardin's for day-old doughnuts.

PRAYER FOR MY SISTER

—C. K. B., 1965–2013

I am bold to say
  I am the shadow,
    she is whole,
      and memory is a mirror
       for me, but for her
        it's more a window
         where she sees us,
          two kids again
           talking under
            water—our floating
             hair, our conversation

in actual bubbles
  popping somewhere
   in the telescopic past
    of a kidney-shaped pool,
     which on scale
      with infinity is still
       rather near where I
        pray, bold to hear
         two voices held
          apart—sending
           messages in waves.

THE GRADUATE GOES TO WORK

I was looking for a middle path
between philosophy and the skinny rain
like glass ants on the elephant ears
and lemon grass that I was, nonetheless,
paid to water. I was building bridges
toward no one's daughter, no one's
idea of a fine lawyer, but I was kind
to the variegated philodendron,
and the boxwoods practically hummed
with being. I was rich with thinking
and thinking about thinking until,
neck-deep in the fertilized azaleas,
I understood that for me it came down
to language, without which
no thinking. Without which no whitefly
incognito, no battalion of beetles
crunching in unison on a soon to be
trucked away longleaf pine. Nothing
saved, nothing noted. Likewise,
I loved to ride the Snapper mower,
and though the turning radius
was tractor-wide, the world made room,
and I hugged the distant shore
of each tree the grass surrounded.

PROCRASTINATION AT DAWN

*The primary imagination I hold to be the living power and prime agent of all
human perception, and as a repetition in the finite mind of the eternal act of
creation in the infinite "I am."*

—S. T. Coleridge

God cues his symphony
    for blue jays and mowers,
        for the mind and the yard
            around it, for the stack

of shingles I've not touched yet
    beneath the walnut tree
        with its webworm net
            regaining the appearance

of reality, performing
    the score of the present,
        for which I am grateful,
            and would not complain.

How cliché to poo-poo
    the boss. And how lucky
        to exist in this body-
            sized space I call my own,

while the work exists
        over there. As with work,
                so with God. Often,
                        between us, an impossible

distance in which great
        measuring is accomplished.
                Would that I could simply
                        visualize climbing

like a cowboy stuntman
        onto the roof, all hammer
                and tool belt, caulking
                        the flashing, patching

what I can before it storms again
        across this, our
                planet, which is also catty-
                        wampus. Apparently,

imagination has its
        limits, plugs no leak,
                though the infinite
                        repeats in the finite

instant, itself a rung
on the ladder to God
where even when I'm not
climbing, I'm climbing.

PAREIDOLIA

Because the brain needs a human world, I see giant faces
in the green shapes that leaves make at the tree line.
One face watches like a minor deity in the Zeus-less pantheon
of my backyard. One stares into the bruised distance
of Picasso's Blue Period. Mighty oak. Persimmon.
Wild Cherry. Black Walnut. How quickly they brim
with self, the trees with their side-eyes and mustaches.
Even when I was a boy kicking the covers, staring out
the window at the myrtle swaying by the streetlight
with its face like the wind-tossed ghost of Ebenezer Scrooge
with pointy beard and monocle, I never wondered,
why faces? Not once did I ask, why not an enormous
saxophone? A banjo? A T-Model Ford? Why not a tree
that looks only like itself? A tree should be enough.

WITH APOLOGIES TO JOHN KEATS

Heard melodies are sweet—cheerleaders giving it hell
    in their pyramid built of team spirit, but sweeter still
        the one time they put me in at quarterback—my best

friend, Scott, open in the end-zone, my rare but perfect spiral
    hitting him on the numbers, his arms outstretched,
        hands practically screaming for the ball—had he not

stepped in a gopher hole and nearly broke his leg. O
    fateful scrimmage, win-less destiny, if Scott
        had caught that pass, would coach have moved us

to second string? Would we have worn jerseys
    at the pep rally instead of slipping out, smoking Merit 100's
        beneath the bleachers? Would we have pumped iron,

bulked up on steroids, gone gung-ho with that one
    taste of touchdown glory? Scott made a banker.
        I make a living teaching poetry. If John Keats

had seen us, he might have said, *Bold QB, never, never*
    canst thou score! And there should definitely be an urn
        for that helmeted instant with me and Scott

suspended on the precipice of athletic success,
    becoming the kind of Bears that strike fear
        into the hearts of Rams and Wildcats, not just

two skinny dudes, bench-warmers who stood
    and yelled on big plays, like a fumble or first down.
        Sophomore year, me and Scott quit the team.

We went to work mowing yards, hauling off
    dead trees, bailing hay, loading water melons
        into tractor trailers. Nobody painted our portrait

on paper, much less on a vase, but here we are, ripe
    for the ages, primed for immortality, my arm
        releasing, the ball tunncling toward him

like a tank-fired missile, Scott defying both sense
    and gravity, his arms extended, fingers spread wide
        as if to catch a different future in his hands.

JANUARY

I go down with gloves and blade to chop
the freeze-blackened branches of the hummingbird bush.
Skeletal, reedy, the branches stick out
like a confusion of car antennas or pelican legs.

Why do so many things in this world look like
so many other things? To keep us from being wrecked
with loss, the Lord gave us likeness?

Hello ocean, meet your twin, the sky.

Just last month, my grandmother, great aunt,
one old neighbor, one new, all passed into a heaven
free of yard tools and the rare
overnight freeze of subtropical North Florida.

Maybe nothing here resembles them.
Maybe semblance is a sucker's participation trophy.
Maybe yard work, like denial, is a stage of grief.

I haul the cut stalks to the firepit
and throw them down like some oversized *I Ching* sticks
that I don't know how to read.
I'm not burning them today.

Nor will I note how smoke through the trees
billows like fog the color of milk
or the scarf of an otherwise invisible horseman.

FIRST PUBLICATION

I passed out in the barracks
after reading the letter. The ambulance
dropped me at Muse Manor.
I was all about the heart monitor,
until they shaved my balls. I called
Gordon Lish on a pay phone.
Thanks for taking the poems, I offered,
I'm in the hospital now. "Send us
some more," he said. I swooned.
Suffice it to say, this was a day of great
swooning. The doctor inquired
if I'd done any drugs. Sure, I said,
quick to add, but not since joining
the Army. I just got my first
poems picked up, I explained,
beaming. He returned with a cup,
commanded me to piss. And this
is what it's like to be famous,
I thought, and shrugged it off, and did
the rest of the week on light duty,
policing the barracks
for spent cartridges and comic strips.

THE WORST WIND

—*Hurricane Michael, 2018*

The day after the hurricane, I realize my battery
      powered toothbrush still vibrates, so I turn on
           the contaminated water
           and get to work. Outside my narrow bathroom window
           the tree line
     is jagged in a new way, the mulberry doubled
         over at the waist, her grand
         and final bow, the downward facing dog
of arboreal adieu. So much
     for the tree house. So much for mulberry wine,
         for spreading
         an old sheet in the grass beneath
the tree and shaking the branches with my daughters,
      separating the fallen berries
           from twigs on white linen, careful to avoid
small spiders. Yea, though I reside
      among the downed
      powerlines and once horizontal strips
      of aluminum siding twisted up and thumped off
like some dinosaur's eyelash, still,
      I have minty, if contaminated, breath. It's hard
not to take it personally, God's protection.

Clearly, I've been chosen. My best
          days and unremembered
acts of kindness
like one-eyed baby dolls standing in line for a bag of ice.

~

Understanding the worst wind is like understanding anything else—I stand
between the mirror and the window and brush my teeth.

Either God has nothing to do with the storm, or God *is* the storm. Or God is
the storm and still has nothing to do with it (the left eye sees not

what the right eye hurricanes). DJ of galaxies, chiropractor of constellations,
I'd rather you weren't involved,

but then what sense
would prayer make? Unless you prefer silence, and poetry

                              more distant from silence and you.

I'll be quiet now, Dear Lord. I'll be real quiet.

~

Quietly, I watched the wind-gusts
from the front porch. A tree snapped, a cracking

like the ropes of a medieval catapult.
God's presence demands

no poem in search of definition, but the sound of the wind
was very much like an ocean,

or the steady traffic of fighter jets.

Holy Boss, stylist of actual stars, accountant
of souls, can't I just hope that you exist?

On one side of the truth, we pilgrim forth.
On the other, we call State Farm,

then prepare for a death minus
the homecoming, minus the sea of angels.

~

The Lord taketh

like a riled-up senator popping a throat button

so that batten flies from his esophagus

and he collapses a little in his toy chair

a beach house flips from its pylons

the ocean like an escaped lunatic

runs naked down HWY 98 pinching herself on the nipples

a pornography of trees

showing all his moves

the glory and the dream

the wind in cahoots

the wind locking the ocean's ankles behind her neck

half yielding to her lover

the ocean cashing it in

the ocean vast and mean

homewrecker weekend

ocean that is not our mother
or is and wants us back

a whole ocean of ocean
the only road into Mexico Beach

where a cadaver dog waits

in a rescue boat

pulling at his leash

~

I didn't know so many trees were hollow in the middle.

I didn't know that a living thing could stand up with dead innards
and still have a great complexion.

If you're keeping a cheek unturned, pilgrim, now's the time to offer it up.

I stayed quiet for a minute for the deceased, the town flat but for the grooves and routes where once stood people, light poles, balconies, widows' peaks, outside sinks for cleaning fish.

I was quiet for the wind, too—plastic and vast, the one wind awesome and frazzled, the wind on fire, the gas-lighting wind, wind of the winged-seed, Shiva and Vishnu, desert wind and oasis wind in a drawn out custody battle, wind that once flowed over the cornfield and grew in the box-fan that sat in my cousin Marylyn's window where it still hums in my memory for no reason I can fathom other than wind, wind in my face when I learned to ride a bike by starting at the top of the hill and building enough speed to stay balanced before crashing into a cyclone fence, wind that wrecks every poet's insufficient boat, wind dressed up and nervous in a field of crooked headstones. But nobody

goes to the wind's funeral.
Most winds don't get a name, Michael.

Nor do most gods get to be God.
Is that what a wind wants? To be somebody?

GREEN OUIJA

If my parents left anything unsaid, they kept it to themselves
before stepping into that breeze that blows backwards,
into that boat that rows beyond passage. If I could hear,
if I could reach their nearest syllable, then I would know

I have assumed the body of the Mississippi Sandhill Crane
I've always wanted to be. If my sisters could fly beside me,
we'd count the teardrop sandbars down the Chickasawhay,
tipping our gray feathers. This is just to say, if the dead

could send a message, it might be written in the cursive
of bees hovering above my uncut grass. If I could read
their flight, I wouldn't need to be satisfied with missing

my father. These are the conditions of the cosmos
and gravity, from which I cannot budge. Meanwhile, airplanes
look like boats motoring overhead, the sky is that deep.

THE BEATLES COME TO MISSISSIPPI: REVOLUTION 9

I jump down in the ditch with a swing blade, the job all to myself, and the ditch is long. The swing blade is dull and the ditch is long and narrow so that half the sweat is not wrecking the blade. I swing at a clump of vines, stirring a cloud of mosquitoes. I swing at mosquitoes. I swing when a moccasin U-turns and the cowbird ignores me. I swing until I see the last haggard stalk at which I swing three times before I throw the blade out of the ditch, pull the damn weed by hand. By God's hand placed there, by my hand chunked into the pile of weeds, vines, and junk raked from ditch to garbage fire before I clock out, pick up my check, bum a ride, bum a cigarette, then unlace my boots in the kitchen where my sister is playing a record backwards to hear the message, because there is a message.

SELF-PORTRAIT AT ONE HUNDRED MILES PER HOUR

You need the camera moving at the same speed
as the '72 Dodge Duster driven by a guy named Pogo
so you can catch me laughing my idiot head off
while my buddy, Pop-tart, pukes into a Slurpee cup.

You need to drive the camera alongside us to see
how ambition runs sideways, let your shutter
click at the rate of hashmarks zipping beneath us
to understand how hilarious not dying can be.

And death is right beside us in a golden bondo'd
El Camino that means to nose ahead, so close
I can't tell whose stereo rocks, "Will you meet me
in the middle, will you meet me in the air?"

The tractor trailer loaded with pulpwood can't help
how fast we're going, nor can the pine trees
flanking the straightaway before the horseshoe turn.
You need to crank the wind up, get a face full

of flash bulb ready for those who will survive.
Like a balloon at a porcupine dance, something pops
in the curve and we limp across the finish line.
Three tires, one rim, back to Ron Spear's garage.

WILLIAM FAULKNER RETURNS TO ADDRESS THE CLASS OF '85

O you who came this far from Corinth, from Buckatunna,
your Mississippi like no other, ole source tit, smack dab
in the un-Harvard of Greene County where three hounds
tree the afterlife in a picture of a forest glued to a building
that used to be a cat house, rule number one: never stand
on a styrofoam cooler. There's plenty on the other side
that you can't find in Pascagoula, but which and where
you are hailing from thus, it never much mattered—if you
can paddle in the wake of your own error, your fish
will be epiphany, and the seagulls your prophets, stitching
salty air above the gambling barges and taffy stands
and tattoo parlors where the flesh becomes word again,
because ever was the voice an echo of the body
as the body is echo of its labor, and I was a short man.

QUESTIONS FROM MY DAUGHTERS

I. WHY DO WE NEED SADNESS?   —ALLI, AGE 14

I think of Son Thomas, bluesman, grave digging understudy
of a one-armed gravedigger. He'd drive down from Leland
and play for us on Fridays when not sculpting human skulls

with river bank clay, sticking in real teeth from a deep jar
he kept on a shelf, shaping a new look for sadness. Sadness
builds the juke joint. Joy cuts the rug. At the Lebanese

diner in Clarksdale at the crossroads, joy and sadness feast
on the same pecan-smoked ribs, then wait by the ditch
for a dude to roll down the window of his Cadillac at midnight,

pedaling glory. But nobody waits for sadness, let alone
with a weirdly tuned guitar and a black cat bone stitched inside
their coat pocket. Why do we need sadness? We don't.

Like weather, sadness just is. Like weather, sadness is what
we're working with, the mojo, the adios, the unforeseen
logos, the tightrope antidote for a snake-bit Mississippi.

II. IS IT SCIENTIFICALLY PROVEN THAT DINOSAURS SAID "ROAR"?

—SOFIA, AGE 13

Not unlike the river that separates
       Vicksburg, Mississippi from Delta,
           Louisiana, home of Daiquiri Stop,

there's a swift gap between Hollywood
       and reality, and yet another between
           what's perceived and what exists

beyond our limits, and this further
       jeopardized by the many layered
           obfuscations of dust. My guess: Giganotosaurus,

ole Claw, ole Three-Finger, coo'd
       like a ten-ton pigeon, a throaty
           welling up from early earth, notes

of root and cave river. A subwoofed
       ululation so righteous it made the horizon
           twitch the way a cow's back

shakes off horseflies. Or maybe its cry
       was in proportion to its brain, the kind
           of refined frequency that steers

bats to mosquitoes, turns a lost
      hound home. Like Chagall's violin,
            like chickens and rain in Patterson,

New Jersey, so much depends on
      distance, how you bridge it, how you climb
            into an ancient skin, sniff around

creek banks and tree tops with a snout
      three feet long, scanning valleys
            through eyes the width of footballs.

How round the day in its pre-fossil
      mist and leafiness, free of drink
            machines and *Teen Vogue*. Where

to go with each star a pilot, each
      corner a cornerstone? Sure as rain,
            sure as the ache for dinner

and friends and home, you have to
      find your register, the sound
            you make, your call, your song.

III. WHY DON'T WE JUST TALK ABOUT POLITICS?

—DARBI, AGE 11

Not the question to ask over family reunion dumplings,
though she means to steer talk away from the Baptist
vs. Episcopal Church. Not wanting to juju the potluck,
I keep my mouth shut. To my right, my uncle,

a Vietnam Vet. To my left, our cousin, raised in England,
gay and proud. O family navigations! O tender steps!
O black and white children singing happy birthday
to the same diabetic grandmother! Here's to taking

none of it for granted, neither u-brown-em rolls
nor turnip greens, not the Lebanese mailman
nor the judge talking hunting dogs with his nephew,
a cannabis farming statistician. We're all here

at the Ag Center, our way forward lit by the match-tips
of history, safest on smooth, on common ground.
So no, we don't talk politics. Unless it's one-on-one.
Unless it's election year. Unless there's beer involved.

Unless it's a bad idea. Unless one leaves a clutch
of campaign signs and bumper stickers in a washtub
by the front door that another, tower of messy
plates in hand, mistakes for a shallow garbage can.

MANGUM LAKE, DROUGHT

For all his talk of nun-chucks and throwing stars, my friend stood watching on the heat-cracked shore when two older kids came screaming up on bikes. One kid put me in a headlock, the other pulled my shoes off and hurled them so far into the gnat-plagued distance that we barely heard the thwack, thwack before both shoes sat in the dung-colored once-lake like paperweights in the Sahara, like hotcakes on a rusty griddle. Once the jerks pedaled off laughing over the hill, my friend came to the rescue. Hang dog, doe-eyed, worm's chin low, bottommost hog's teat decumbent, he held out his own sneakers, twin boats of fungus and funk, shoestrings the color of mop water, but I did not sit down. I did not put them on. I chunked them into the bald nothing, into the arid, pathless crater of that no-swim swimming hole. Who else among us deserves forgiveness?

ELEGY FOR HELLO

Because I am a Leo,
I take things personally,
as when the cashier at Walmart
starts running the pork loin
over the bar code reader
without saying hello, and so I
say hello, which seems like
an insult at this late point
in our otherwise silent
interaction, a hurtful hello.
A judgmental hello. I get
that ours is a meeting of
primarily commercial import,
but what's a hello cost?
Then I think, maybe she's just
done with hello. Maybe she's
saving hello for her four-year old
whom she will pick up
from the daycare that costs
two week's wages before
driving home to the water drip
around the living room
light fixture. On the other
hand, maybe she's just roughing it
and after work she'll drive

her Benz to Golden Eagle
where she'll report on her day
whilst sipping a cocktail
with a slice of grapefruit
at the 9th hole clubhouse.
I worked the register
at Greer's, served a tour or two
at Sac-N-Save, and unless I
was toting a leaning tower
of frozen pizzas from the walk-in
and couldn't see you through
my frozen glasses, I
said hello. Likewise, I said
hello to the Walmart cashier
whose nametag read "Smile
JOYCE Our People Make
the Difference!" and mine wasn't
a hello that says, what the hell,
Joyce, can't you see me
standing here with my unchecked
tater-tots being a human
amongst humans in a somewhat
dehumanizing warehouse
jam packed with jeans,
wrist watches, frozen hamburger,

televisions, live crabs? No,
mine was a friendly hello.
And Joyce looked up and smiled
and said hello back, and we
both relaxed a little, and I
quit trying to imagine her life
beyond the conveyer belt
that inched my items toward her hand
until she passed them, one
by one, over the red laser.

IN DEFENSE OF STOICISM

My love, the waiting room of Radiology Associates
with its post-industrial art gallery vibe
replete with diecast warehouse ducts
does little to assuage my estimate
of the pain that you might endure when the needles
come out and they poke at the nodule
in your throat from six different angles.
Though I'm rooms away, I try
to be cool so you'll relax, that you might
not flinch, that the needles won't pinch
or burn, won't find anything super
unusual, won't leave you reeling from the un-
expected warmth of a porcupine scarf.
If I were to be honest, I'd fall apart.
Therefore, I revoke my worst worry
and we will never be separate for more
than the seventy-two hours it takes
for you to indulge in a girl's weekend
with your old friends at Shell Point.
I visualize health: I see the sweat
on the cold beer we share by a pool
with our respective novels, their pages' corners
darkened a bit by suntan lotion

fingerprints. I see grandkids and canoe trips
down the Sopchoppy and a red Dodge
at the boat ramp on Mount Beasor Road.
Weddings, of course, and graduations.
And even if I sometimes see you and me
with bad hips and the same arthritis
that our grandparents endured,
I see us happy, nonetheless, not worried
about biopsies or sickness or chemo
fatigue, fingers too numb to work
pajama buttons.
     I welcome the calm
sweeping in through the brash light
of the waiting room's wall-sized window,
noon sun glaring off the parking lot
with its short, newly planted trees.
Inside, the lobby chair is stiff, not made
to lean back, so in my mind it's a puffed-up recliner
where a person can find some relief
waiting for their name to be called, or for the one
they love to return with a bag of ice
nestled between clavicle and chin.

STANZAS FROM EARTH

Like clothespins on a hearse curtain,
                         my jerry-rigged funeral will continue
                         without me.
As for my point of view, pondering of themes I love best—night, sleep, junkshop
                         guitars, telepathic wheat,
                         sheet metal chicken coops
                         in the backyards of West Jackson—
Surely, I will fly with invisible crows over the valley of the Provine Rams.
Surely, I will step through chain link, paying no one.

Like a mandolin in a bone tree, like a back hoe in the opera lobby,
                         like a snot rag in a jewelry shop,
                         like magnets in a dog collar,
                         like cocktails at the courthouse,
I'll feel out of place early on,
the wind barbed between my ears transparent,
                         squirrelly void of my impersonal space.

~

You won't see me sitting on the fire hydrant at Capital and Calhoun, or in the
       vacant lot beside the Stop & Go.
You won't see Wanda bring Ronnie some Now & Laters, or Quint picking his
       fro out, supernatural.
You won't see Doug J. with enough empty Coke bottles for a Hormel half-can
       and a bag of Fritos.
Unless you're standing in front of a mirror, you won't see yourself waiting at
       the no-bench bus stop marked by a narrow sign on a telephone pole.

Somewhere east of eyeshot, carrying the Gulf of Mexico in my plastic spoon,
talking politics with my old man in a spider web hammock,
cutting pearl inlay for a snowflake's tombstone . . .

I'd rather not swim to the other side of any river, nor ferry on a current of inadequate,
overly earnest, embarrassed, if not outright apologetic metaphor
incapable of disguising its own fear, transforming nothing.

But death draws the long straw, just as the afterlife
                         rides shotgun with its beautiful face in the wind.

~

My sister died at 48, my other sister too—I'm pushing 49, sweet momma,
　　　called the 48 blues.
Yea though I drag a muddy boot through the gates of non-duality, if I clean
　　　up, sweet momma, can I stay all night with you?
I may not be the infinite rebate on the eternal Calgon coupon in the finite
　　　Jitney Jungle,
and maybe I'm not the midnight moth-light over Hardy Junior High, Pecan
　　　Boulevard, and the Vo-Tech Center,
but sure as the ancient, one-eyed barber at Capital Cuts knows me as my
　　　father's son,
I will jump the Mississippi Coliseum on a bored-out Huffy, surfing the
　　　plywood ramp for you, sweet momma.
I'll wheelie over the volcano's mouth even as it blows spit bubbles, leaving in
　　　my wake a constellation of Red Hots.
Sure as a mirror catches from nowhere my bicycle breath, if I clean up,
　　　sweet momma, can I look back at you?
Can I hold your hand by the concession stand in three hundred years?
If I show up at your square dance, will you call my tune? step to my
　　　number? gauge my particle levels?
Will your heart make room for me the way a curtain billows imperceptibly
　　　when a jet thunders over?
If you can't hold me, what's all this loving for?
I don't need a monolith. I need a mojo hand.
　　　　　　If I can't come in, sweet momma, let me sit down in your door.

ACKNOWLEDGMENTS

My sincere gratitude to the editors of the following journals, in which poems in this book (sometimes in different versions) first appeared:

About Place: "West Jackson Topography"; *American Journal of Poetry*: "First Day Middle School," "Self-Portrait as Thief Confessing after the Fact," "Spacetime Blues," and "Stanzas from Earth"; *Apalachee Review*: "Questions from My Daughters" and "The Worst Wind"; *Banyan Review*: "In Defense of Stoicism"; *DIAGRAM*: "Flea Trap" and "Prayer for My Sister"; *Electric Literature: The Commuter*: "The Law of Truly Large Numbers"; *Fogged Clarity*: "Group Meditation, Camp Bratton-Green, 1978"; *Grass Routes*: "Green Ouija" and "Procrastination at Dawn"; *Jet Fuel Review*: "Good Grief"; *New South*: "The Beatles Come to Mississippi: Revolution 9"; *Nightjar*: "Easy Now"; *Rhino*: "Portrait of Sadie in Three Worlds"; *River Styx*: "Meditation on a Bowl Made from a Tree Upended in Last Year's Hurricane" and "Watching NASCAR on the Anniversary of My Sister's Death"; *Saw Palm*: "A Day in September"; *Sheila-Na-Gig online*: "Making a Sandwich for Mikhail Baryshnikov"; *Snakebird Anthology: Anhinga Press*: "Decoupage" and "Pareidolia"; *Southern Indiana Review*: "January" and "Portrait of Child as City Planner"; *Washington Square Review*: "The Graduate Goes to Work"; *Willow Springs*: "First Publication."

Thank you, especially, to the Guggenheim Foundation, the National Endowment for the Arts, Florida State University's Committee for Faculty Research, and the Florida Arts Commission for fellowships and funding that provided inestimable support toward the completion of this book.

Thanks also to the trusted friends, poets, and writers who have helped this book and its poet along in myriad and invaluable ways: Gbenga Adesina, Tacey Atsitty, Ruth Baumann, Collin Callahan, Kerry James Evans, Yolanda Franklin, Juan Carlos Galeano, Tanya Grae, Ian Haight, Rodney Jones, Jude Jordan, Dave Killeen, Max Lasky, Zuleyha Ozturk, Michelle Liles, Davis McCombs, Marda Messick, Jedd McFatter, C. Liegh McInnis, Travis Mossotti, Robert Herschbach, Zachary Scott, Jeffrey Skinner, Steve G. Smith, and Jane Springer.

And special thanks to my wife, first-reader, and partner in perpetual adventure, Jami McFatter Kimbrell.